THE AUTHORITY GUIDE TO
TRUSTED
SELLING

Building stronger, deeper and more profitable
relationships with your customers to create lifetime loyalty

PAUL AVINS

The Authority Guide to Trusted Selling

Building stronger, deeper and more profitable relationships with your
customers to create lifetime loyalty

© Paul Avins

ISBN 978-1-909116-77-1
eISBN 978-1-909116-78-8

Published in 2016 by Authority Guides
authorityguides.co.uk

Printed in the United Kingdom.

Contents

Paul Avins is our trusted mentor, business coach, sales expert and all round good bloke – you should buy this book, heck you should buy all his books – each one is full of nuggets of business wisdom that will get you through your toughest day.

Nicola Whiting
COO Titania Group

Foreword

If you're standing in an airport or bookshop, or reading an Amazon preview (trying to make a purchasing decision) then I've created a shortcut below – just for you…

For those who aren't currently skipping to the tills, or folks like me who like to read the foreword (before getting to the 'juicy bits') this is how Titania met Paul and why we think this book will make a difference, to *you*.

Paul initially attracted us to his F12 business leaders and entrepreneurs event with a cunning ploy – he showed genuine and persistent interest in our future success.

Titania had won a series of awards for product excellence, so he wrote to us saying 'people who enter and win awards tend to be people focused on growth and taking positive steps' and 'we were the sort of people he liked to work with'. He included an event invite that offered a 'no pitch' promise, networking and food (so he had all our boxes ticked) but we weren't sure whether we wanted to go – so we ignored him.

Thankfully Paul employs his own methods and followed up with a perfectly pitched call – that cinched it. We spent more time talking than he did – he really actively *listened* and reflected back a clear understanding of what we wanted for our business.

We found ourselves agreeing to attend, we're very glad we did.

Paul builds *trust* like no other leadership coach we've ever encountered.

This book is a shortcut to a better understanding of your clients and potential clients; it's a 'trusted selling' programme that is hugely powerful.

Applying its principles generated successes for Titania such as:

- Tripling event attendance to a key seminar
- Doubling our lead generation at a competitive trade show
- Increasing our sales team engagement (as they have more productive client conversations)

Providing clients the *type* of information they need, when they need it and delivering it in the best format for them – is the key to successful sales and marketing.

We buy from people we know, like and trust – in today's information rich 'instant' society, we can't just mail out a brochure and hope for the best. We have to build quality, long-term, *trusted* relationships that provide mutual benefit for both parties.

If you want to give better service and build deeper, stronger and more profitable relationships with your clients, then dip into these pages frequently, take action and explore their concepts fully – when applied, they will radically transform your business.

Nicola Whiting

Introduction

Let me ask you a few questions as we get started together.

- Have you ever been *frustrated* by your customer not seeing the value your product or services can deliver to them?
- Do you ever find it *difficult* to contact, connect and convert certain types of prospect or buyer?
- Is your company *suffering* from outdated 'pressure' selling techniques and a belief that if you just make more calls you are guaranteed to hit your sales targets?

If you answered 'yes' to any of these questions, I know how you feel. In my more than 25 year career in various sales roles, whether employed, self-employed or as a business owner, I've often experienced the same either personally or with clients.

Let me be clear: I've always loved selling since I first sold my Smurfs to my sister when I was just eight years old. I've always seen it as an opportunity to solve problems for people and a way to serve, add value and build a long-term relationship.

But the world is changing.

Today customers have more access to information online about our companies, products and services and what real customers think of them, having purchased and used them.

Often when we meet a potential client they will know a lot about our products' features and benefits as well as all our competitors.

Then there are social platforms like LinkedIn, Twitter and Facebook that let them see what type of person we are, which people we have in common and how we express ourselves and interact with others.

To me, most traditional sales training feels 'at odds' with our current reality. However, this creates a huge opportunity for those of us able to move away from the obsessive focus on sales techniques and move towards a value led approach built on a foundation of high trust.

When you make this shift, and I'll explain exactly how to in this book, you can experience results like one of my F12 Mastermind clients in the garden design and landscaping market.

The owner wanted to grow their sales, as most of my clients do, and asked me to train her team in high trust selling. Now I'm a great believer, as you'll find out, in understanding people and tapping into their natural abilities to build rapport and trust. I'm also a big believer in tracking the return on investment (ROI) from any training programme myself or my team delivers.

Here's what's interesting.

Before the training they had an average order value (AOV) of between £15,000 and £20,000. Now, after applying what I'll share with you over the next few chapters this nearly *doubled* in just 90 days. Which was a great result for them, but the story gets even better as they also landed their first ever £100,000 contract.

Now am I guaranteeing you the same results?

No of course I can't, as I don't know your market, company, product or experience; however, I can tell you that this is not a unique story from a client and that this selling approach can deliver significant results and returns for you, but you have to *apply* it.

This book is for you if you are:

- a salesperson on the road selling products or services
- a telemarketer wanting more results from the same effort
- a sales manager wanting to get more sales from your team
- a sales director looking to build a high trust sales culture
- a business owner or entrepreneur selling your idea to investors
- a coach, trainer or consultant selling yourself and your skills
- a service professional like accountant, lawyer or human resources (HR) professional
- looking to go into sales and want to start with proven best practices.

So let me be clear: it is possible to make more sales, with less effort and build stronger, deeper and more profitable relationships with your clients.

This Authority Guide will show you exactly how with the Dynamic Selling System™.

Before we dive into the content I wanted to share with you a statistic that really shocked me.

Bridge Group Inc. in the USA found that companies typically spend between $10,000 and $15,000 to hire a new salesperson, yet they typically invest less than $2,000 per year training them to succeed.

That just blows my mind and makes me want to congratulate you on downloading or picking up this book to invest in yourself.

The greatest investment you can ever make, in my view, is to invest in yourself. I remember years ago being told by a speaker from stage that if you wanted to make more sales, then invest 10 per cent of everything you earn back in developing your sales skills. For the last 25 years I've been doing this and I can tell you that the return on this investment has been the highest of anything I've invested in, including businesses, people and property.

As I often say in my workshops – the more you learn the more you earn.

So if there is only one action you take from this book, and I hope there will be a lot more, then commit now to invest 10 per cent back in *your* personal development. After all, your future sales success depends on it.

Here's a quick overview of what you'll learn in the next few pages:

- Why this new trusted sales approach can triple your sales
- Why trust beats tips, tricks and tactics every time
- Why being in flow will help your sales to grow
- What the four dynamic selling energies are and how to spot them

- What buyers really look for in a trusted advisor versus a product pusher
- Who buys on new ideas, who buys on relationships, who buys when the time is right and who needs lots of detail to buy
- When the perfect time is to follow up for higher conversions
- When you can move forward at speed with a new client and when you need to go slow to secure the sale
- How to position yourself as *the* trusted advisor in your market
- How to structure your presentation for maximum positive impact with each of the four buyer energies
- How to generate more referrals from each type of buyer
- How to accelerate your sales results while working less hours

As you can see, we have plenty to get stuck into together, so let's jump right in and let me tell you a story about when I learned the ultimate sales lesson.

Every sale has five basic obstacles...

No need, no money, no hurry, no desire or no trust.

Zig Ziglar

The ultimate sales lesson

Many years ago, having dropped out of university to stop learning and start earning (big mistake looking back), I started my career in sales working with my father in the family business.

He wanted me to understand the customers and the products and felt going out selling was the best way to teach me this knowledge and the skills needed to succeed.

Like many companies I work with now there was no formal sales training or induction to set me up for success. I was just given a map of my area, a list of customers and some potential customers and my car keys and told to go out and make sales and hit my targets. Perhaps you can relate to this?

Back then I didn't have the luxury or leverage of my own mobile phone to help make appointments, as the one my dad had was still the size of a brick and cost a small fortune. How times have changed for the better.

Now I was lucky enough to be introduced to the world of personal and self-development. As a result I started listening to tapes while I drove to see clients, yes before CDs or iPods, from top sales trainers and motivational speakers like Zig Ziglar, Anthony Robbins and Tom Hopkins.

Quick aside – this was when I first decided I wanted to be a sales trainer, as back then the business coaching industry had not even reached the UK.

Back to my story. What I realised was the speakers in their own way were all saying the same thing.

Stop asking the question, 'How can I make more sales?' Start asking, 'How can I add more *value* before the sale so that I'm seen as a trusted advisor by the customer?'

This question changed my selling life forever, years before any books were even written on the subject of trust-based selling. It's been responsible for me generating hundreds of millions of pounds in sales and profits, not just for my family business back then, but in industries as diverse as domestic security, digital marketing services, IT services, horticulture, domestic cleaning, coaching, consulting and business training to name a few of the companies I have run over the last 25 years.

Let me put it simply to you: the formula shown in Figure 1 just works.

What I have set out to do in this book is to show you how to spot a buyer's buying energy so that you can gain their trust by adding value in a way they recognise.

What's key is that you understand that value has to be recognised; we all generate and identify it differently based on our personal profile and energy.

Figure 1 How to increase sales and profits

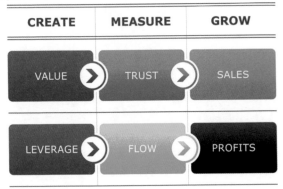

Copyright Talent Dynamics

As you'll learn as you go through this book, for some people ideas, innovation and problem solving adds value. For others it's all about relationships and connectivity through people in their network.

Some people see value in reliability and getting things done or to market at the right time. After all, if you were to try to sell red roses on 15 February you'd have a tough time no matter how good a 'closer' you are, as you missed the time when the product added the most value.

Finally, there are those who see value in the detail, data and expertise in specific areas that they can leverage to be more efficient and effective.

I hope that learning and applying this information makes you as excited as I have been in wanting to share it with you, as I know what it's done for me personally and professionally.

In fact, I would go so far as to say it can triple your sales and in the next chapter I'll prove it to you.

There are only three times you can build
trust with a prospect or customer:

1) Before the sales call
2) During the sales call
3) After the sales call

Dean Jackson

Why this approach could triple your sales

OK, it's a big claim in a world full of marketing and sales hype and empty promises; however, there is some strong science and maths behind my claim so stay with me.

The truth is that most salespeople sell in the way that *they* like to buy.

Stop and think about that for a moment. In fact, think about a time in the recent past where you purchased an item for say over £1,000. Think about the salesperson that helped you with that buying decision: were they like you? Did they sell to you in the way you like to buy?

Did you find yourself thinking, 'I like this person; they really get me and what I need'?

It's not really a shocking insight I'll grant you, but I'll bet it's been true in your sales career that there have been some people you instantly connected with, or had rapport with.

Then there are other types of people who you just don't seem to be able to break through to, connect with or close and all your usual sure-fire strategies just fall on deaf ears.

You leave meetings frustrated, knowing that your product or service could have solved their problem and really helped them.

But imagine if you could quickly and easily tell what type of buyer you were dealing with, the way they liked to be communicated with, their sales triggers that get them to take action and the deal dangers that could stop your sale in its tracks.

Armed with this information and insight, I would suggest that you could significantly increase your conversion rates.

In fact, if there are four distinct buying energies and you naturally sell to one of them that means your conversion rate may be just 25 per cent. As some people have a mix of two energies, which I'll come on to in Why trust beats tips, tricks and tactics, my experience is that a large number of salespeople average around the 35 per cent conversion rate, but for this example we'll work with 25 per cent.

Of course there are always exceptions to this and some will be a lot higher and some a lot lower. Do you know your current cold closing rate? If not, I strongly suggest you start to track it if you want to be successful in this profession.

Back to my 300 per cent increase claim.

If you are at the 25 per cent level, that means you close one in four of the brand new leads you see. I'm excluding repeat customer meetings as your conversion rate on these should be far higher, closer to the 90 per cent level, and will distort the numbers if included.

By the time you've read through this Authority Guide you'll know more about how to connect, communicate and convert all four of the buying energies than 99 per cent of the other salespeople out there.

That's a huge competitive advantage for you.

So if you were able to open relationships (I hate the term closing as it implies pressure to get someone to do something) with the other three out of four or 75 per cent of buyers you would, in essence, triple your sales.

Table 1 The Dynamic Selling Multiplier

Customer	You	You + 3
Dynamo Energy	✓	✓
Blaze Energy		✓
Tempo Energy		✓
Steel Energy		✓

It may be slightly unrealistic to win every new potential client you meet, but I have clients who, using this system, are achieving levels of 90 per cent+ when they meet with a correctly qualified buyer.

Whatever your current level of sales success, the Dynamic Selling System™ will magnify your results, pure and simple.

If you wanted to take it beyond just the selling process, you can start to create four different marketing funnels and four different types of brochure, each one appealing to the different buying energies main drivers. But more on that in later chapters.

For now the key question becomes, 'What can stop this working for you?'

Two words – beliefs and identity.

In the next chapter I'm going to help you uncover the three biggest areas salespeople have limiting beliefs about, and which impact their identities and stop them achieving their goals – and how to break through them.

Beliefs, baggage and breakthroughs

We all live in the same world, with the same 24 hours, the same learning resources like blogs and podcasts, the same social media platforms and the same Internet.

The only thing stopping us from achieving our sales goals, targets and dreams is the stories we choose to tell ourselves about why we can't. Let's be clear: we all *choose* to buy into stories, either our own, our managers' or perhaps our parents' story about what they felt we were capable of achieving.

When it comes to selling, your baggage and beliefs can literally drag you to the bottom like an anchor.

So how do you uncover these sometimes positive, but more likely negative, limits we all have buried in our subconscious mind?

The answer is to ask yourself questions that bypass the conscious mind where our 'rational lies' are being told to help us feel good. If you want to jump to the next level, and I'm assuming you do or we would not be on this journey together, then you have to tap the dark recesses of your mind and 'get real' with yourself.

If you're not familiar with your subconscious, this is how it works. When you learn to drive a car, for example, you are programming your subconscious mind with repetition and the new driving program sticks. Today you can drive almost on autopilot, drink coffee and listen to the radio all at the same time. If this program was not installed in your subconscious mind, you would have to relearn how to drive a car every time you got into one.

This is also the same with your selling beliefs and habits.

Let's get started by identifying the programs you already have installed, as it's the first step in moving towards breaking through the ones that no longer serve you. I'm about to take you through three powerful questions. You need to limit your answers to just 90 seconds. If you want to have me personally coach you through this, then go to

www.paulavins.com/beliefbreakthroughs where I have put a blog post with a short video and worksheet you can download.

I already know that some of you reading this will have the profile type that says, 'I'll come back and do this later. I want to crack on with what's next.' If that's you, *stop*. It takes less than five minutes to really understand what you believe impacts your sales results.

Question 1: *What comes into your mind when I say 'salesperson'?*

You have 90 seconds to keep writing and get everything down … and stop.

Question 2: *What comes into your mind when I say 'customers'?*

You have 90 seconds to keep writing and get everything down … and stop.

Question 3: *What comes into your mind when I say 'money'?*

You have 90 seconds to keep writing and get everything down … and stop.

It's now time to reflect and review what you wrote down. When we run this exercise as part of our trusted sales training days, we find people are surprised by some of the answers they put down.

So how about you?

When I asked you to think about a 'salesperson', what came to mind? Usually the responses fall into two categories, negative or positive. I've listed some of the most common responses below.

Negative:

- Pushy
- Loud
- Self-interested
- Talkative
- Money focused
- Flashy
- Obnoxious
- High pressure
- Doesn't listen
- Insincere
- Liar
- Dishonest
- Lazy
- Greedy
- Disorganised
- Selfish
- Aggressive
- Money grabbing

Positive:

- Driven
- Hard-working
- Sets goals
- Problem solver
- Persistent
- Friendly
- Good listener
- Passionate
- Focused
- Outgoing
- Funny
- Coachable
- Positive
- Resourceful
- Knowledgeable
- Winners

If you had any or many of the negatives beliefs, do you see a problem? If your subconscious knows this is how you view salespeople and how most of your prospective customers view you, how do you think you'll perform in the role?

Perhaps you had more from the positive list on the right? That's fantastic, but watch out as spending too much time around negative people outside or inside sales can rub off and we don't want that for you do we?

So let's go on to question number 2.

What came to mind when I asked you to think about customers?

Again here are some of the most common responses for you to compare with.

Negative:

- Annoying
- Disloyal
- Hard work
- Liars
- Difficult
- Price shoppers
- Frustrating

Positive:

- Driven
- Friendly
- Loyal
- Positive
- Fun
- Knowledgeable
- Valuable
- Trusting

On which side did you come down in favour?

Think about it. If your job involves spending time with people you don't like, value or appreciate at a subconscious level, do you think potential customers may just pick up on that energy through your voice, actions and body language?

Totally. You know when somebody is genuinely interested in serving you when you walk into a shop, and when they couldn't care less if you buy or not. So negative beliefs about customers are a huge subconscious sales prevention energy.

My questions to you: 'If you do have more negatives than positives, are you even selling to the right market or customers? Who are you passionate about spending time around day to day? What industries sell to those people and can you go and work for companies in that market?'

Your time, life and energy is just too precious to waste in a role that does not motivate you, and your results will reflect it. As I often say, passion leaves before profit in a business and it's the same for salespeople.

Last but not least, we have the question about your beliefs about money.

This is a topic that many salespeople find uncomfortable to talk about, as it can bring up beliefs passed down to them by parents, politicians or priests. Yet it's so important, as we are going to need to talk to people about money as part of our role with customers.

Let's take a quick look at some of the typical responses we see during our training days.

Negative:

- Does not grow on trees
- Dirty
- Hard to get
- Limited amount
- Difficult to earn
- Never enough
- Life is hard
- Evil
- Rich people are greedy
- Debts
- Brings problems
- Struggle
- Changes people

Positive:

- Abundant
- Limitless
- Positive
- Fun to spend
- Invest
- Valuable
- Flows to me
- Easy to make
- Deserve it
- Powerful tool
- Resource
- Motivator
- Reward

Can you see how the negative beliefs can block your sales success? After all, if you think money is hard to make, there is never enough, and rich, successful people are greedy, then imagine how you'll behave during a sales negotiation with somebody successful.

It's not going to be an energetic match and, more importantly, they will not trust you on a gut level even if your product or service is a great match for them.

This is because money is just an idea backed by confidence.

Here's a story to demonstrate.

I had a client whose salespeople were selling very high-end home entertainment systems to wealthy clients at home. The problem was that when the business owner went out to visit potential customers, he always converted them and at very high average order values of over £50,000, while his sales team struggled to convert 20 per cent, and when they did their values were down 50 per cent at £25,000.

He had tried traditional sales training models like SPiN and plenty of product training, but with no result. What we uncovered was that his salespeople, on average, only made £45,000 at best per year. They just could not get their heads around why or how anybody could afford to spend more than they made in 12 months on a home entertainment system, so either felt intimidated or simply discounted like crazy to try to get the sale.

To fix this situation, we hired two new salespeople used to making over £100,000 a year, sent them out to all these leads and gave the lower quality leads to the existing team. With bigger beliefs, experiences and identities that supported them, their conversion rates were closer to 65 per cent, with average order values in the £40,000 to £45,000 range. Still a fraction below the owner, but that was to be expected as he was one of the best sales communicators I've ever met, plus he had the credibility of being the business owner as well to seal the deal with clients.

Now that we know what your limiting beliefs and identities are, we need to move on to step two and ask, 'What is keeping these limiting beliefs in place for you?'

Usually a belief comes from an experience or repeated experience that acts as evidence that it's true. It's key here to understand that on some level you are gaining something, however odd that may sound, or you would not be holding on to this belief.

Perhaps it gives you a reason or excuse for not hitting your targets and succeeding?

Whatever your reason, the next step in shifting this belief is to look for evidence against it. For example, if your belief is, 'It's hard to make money selling these products to my customers as we are just too expensive.' Yes, this one often comes up from salespeople. The reframe game begins by asking, 'Is there anybody else in your company, team or industry currently making a lot of money selling products like yours to customers like yours?' Of course the answer is *yes*.

Once your brain can accept that there is a different reality and it is possible, all you need to do is convince your subconscious that it's possible for you as well.

This is all about learning to trust yourself and to trust your subconscious mind by reprogramming it, just like you would need reprogramming with new driving skills if you wanted to start racing cars or you wanted to learn to fly a plane. Your old programs don't help with this, so your mental software needs to be upgraded.

The best way to do this is with *afformations* – in essence, powerful questions designed to refocus your subconscious on the solutions you want as opposed to the problems or challenges you may be experiencing.

Let me give you a few examples:

N = Why do I always miss my sales targets? (Very negative belief question.)

P = Why do I find it so easy and fun to make sales and win new business?

N = Why do I find it so hard to win new business?

P = Why does everybody I speak to want to buy from me?

N = Why does everybody seem to reject me and my products?

P = Why am I so good at attracting ideal clients who see my value and trust me?

Take a look at the three pairs of questions. Which ones make you feel more positive and optimistic just by reading them?

The second ones. This is the key: your mind will go to work to *answer* these questions as it's a supercomputer. Your job is to start giving it a new set of programs and its job is not to question them, but to run them.

I know, sounds too easy right? Well here's the hard part – *you* have to keep repeating them for 30/60/90 days, even when it feels uncomfortable and crazy, until you start to experience feeling different, which will cause you to take different actions. Then, when you take the right action, you get the right results (Figure 2).

Figure 2 The Question Accelerator

One of my mindset mentors, Noah St John, has in my view written the definitive book on this subject and you can download a free copy at www.paulavins.com/afformations

When you start to positively program your sales subconscious you'll really start to trust yourself to make great sales decisions, great offers and great contacts, and this in turn will help others to trust you.

Why trust beats tips, tricks and tactics

We live in a world where everybody is rushed off their feet, over-run by 'to-do' lists and desperate to catch up with all the social updates they are plugged into.

However, this has created a problem as more and more of us look for silver bullet solutions or quick fixes so that we can get fast results and move on to the next problem on our list.

Marketers promise these in their copy, appealing to the reptilian part of our brain. We willingly trade proven concepts in favour of the latest tips and tricks, just to get more clients over the line so that we can hit our targets and feel less in fear of losing our jobs, businesses or lifestyles.

The truth, though, is that these quick fix solutions never last, and while they may win you the odd deal or two they ultimately leave us feeling empty, unfulfilled and looking for a better, longer lasting approach.

That approach is all about building *trust*, the commodity most lacking in our world today. We don't trust the media, we don't trust the banks anymore and we certainly don't trust the politicians, so why in the world would we trust a salesperson who is clearly only interested in their commission?

But the truth is somewhat different.

Researchers from the University of Houston, the Singapore Management University and the Department of Management Science and Systems, State University of New York found that:

1. Trust was the strongest predictor of a consumer's purchase intention

2. Followed by perceived benefit of the product or service

3. Followed by level of personal risk (potential to lose money, time or face).

So trust is the number one predictor of intention to buy, assuming of course the consumer is interested in the product you have to offer and it solves a problem for them.

In fact typically what you find in business-to-business selling situations is that buyers are looking at four key areas when they are making their decision.

First they will look at the actual product or service you are putting in front of them.

- Will it deliver a real solution to the business?
- Does it have the features to be a valuable solution?

But this is only 50 per cent of what they are looking at; depending on their buying dynamics, these can be more important. However, today's buyers are also looking at:

- Is this company going to be a good partner for us long term?
- Is their salesperson, as a trusted advisor, offering value and expertise (Figure 3)?

Figure 3 Four things buyers look for in sales presentations

Product	People
Right features	Right company/partner
Valuable solution	Trusted advisor

What I find fascinating is that the benefits of the product will only sway a prospect's intention to buy if they think there is a low risk of loss and the benefits outweigh that perceived risk. This is all down to how the salesperson communicates with them during the sales process.

If they don't trust the company, salesperson or the product claims, no amount of 'big bold benefits', as one sales trainer I know likes to call them, are likely to induce them to buy.

There you have it: trust is an essential component of any sale, even if your features and benefits hit the spot.

So how exactly do you get prospects and customers to trust you?

The perfect place to start is by understanding your unique Triangle of Trust (Figure 4) and the skills and knowledge you need to acquire to be seen as a trusted advisor.

Figure 4 Triangle of Trust™

As you can see from Figure 4, there are three main ways you can build trust with customers. This is vital to your success and needs to happen before you jump into product demonstrations, features, facts and so on.

Let's walk you through each area so you understand how to implement it into your sales calls and can better answer the question every customer has thought, 'Why should I trust you?'

First we have your *credibility*.

This is made up of three distinct parts:

- Your personal credibility
- Your products' credibility
- Your company's credibility

It would be nice to think they all shared the impact equally, but in my experience your personal credibility will be responsible for 50 per cent of your score.

That can be a challenge for some people, especially if you live in a culture that has taught you not to 'brag' about what you've done so you don't offend anybody. However, I'll show you why that no longer holds as much truth in today's social media and celebrity driven culture.

There is a lot of depth behind these three areas and this is just one of the key exercises we take salespeople through on our trusted sales training days.

For more information on these, visit www.paulavins.com/salestraining where you can download a free video explaining the Triangle of Trust™ in more detail.

Let's move on to how you can personally get more into your unique Sales Flow™.

Let your customer determine your sales
presentation style.

Anthony Robbins

The four sales dynamic energies

The fundamental belief that guides us is that different customers need to be prospected, presented to and managed differently.

They are not the same and don't buy in the same way, so treating them all the same in your sales presentation is a huge waste of time, energy and sales opportunity.

We probably all know that intuitively, yet somehow sales training has never evolved to reflect the fact that with a lot of the tools that are available in the marketplace today, we can be much more sophisticated in our approaches, much more refined at building rapport and connecting with clients.

Let's get started with the tool we use called Talent Dynamics, which has been taken by over 500,000 people around the world. Created by Roger Hamilton, it's a unique mix of East and West philosophy and tools seamlessly blended together.

We use Talent Dynamics because while it may initially look like just another profiling tool, such as DiSC® or Insights®, it's far more than that.

It is a framework that allows you to tune in to where and how trust is generated with customers in a sales situation.

It will also help you to understand why certain parts of the sales cycle feel effortless and easy for you (sales flow) and why others are a real challenge and often cause the most issues with customers.

If you are a sales manager or business owner trying to manage salespeople, this information is vital as it ensures you have the right people in the right sales roles doing the right activities that generate more leverage and profits for the company.

Figure 5 The Talent Dynamics Square and the eight profiles

There are four main energies, or frequencies, within Talent Dynamics: Dynamo, Blaze, Tempo and Steel (Figure 5) and 8 Profiles. Starting at the top these are Creator, Star, Supporter,

Deal Maker, Trader, Accumulator, Lord and finally Mechanic. All of the profiles have elements of other energies to differing levels.

We will start with understanding three things:

1. Knowing yourself
2. Knowing your customer
3. Knowing your team

When you understand yourself first, how you like to naturally sell, then understanding how to change your approach depending on the type of buyer you're in front of, will help you to build more rapport.

Imagine you were trying to sell to a customer who only spoke Japanese. It would be a very difficult task if you only spoke English. This is how it can feel for a Tempo energy customer being sold to by a high Dynamo sales person like a Creator profile.

The key to making more sales is to learn to 'speak' their energy or language, which is what this book will teach you.

Obviously you can't have a buyer take a profile test before you go and see them, although we have had some clients who are selling multimillion pound deals actually do that as part of the process, which has been hugely effective.

What we will do is give you a set of trust building strategies you can use to help you identify somebody's primary energy. Then you'll be able to alter your approach to resonate with them at a much deeper level.

It's important to understand that this is not about manipulation; it's all about deeper communication and rapport with the customer. This way you are better able to serve them and help them to solve their unique problems as a trusted advisor.

In some shocking customer research recently, only 13 per cent of customers believed a salesperson could accurately understand their needs. That's why getting them to trust you is such a key skill.

Once you have a customer's trust the skill is to add real value to them and to let go of the need to push for the sale. It's one of the reasons I hate sales trainers who still teach "ABC" Always Be Closing – nobody responds to that any more!

Think of it like dating, some customers will have problems you can really help solve and some will not be right for you. Your skill is to ask great questions to find out what their real issues are and to help them see if you have a solution that fits. If not, be happy to move onto your next 'date'. They will feel great about you and your company because you added genuine value to them even though they didn't purchase from you there and then.

A study done by Gartner research found that 67% of customers who don't buy from you today will come back to you if they felt you had their best interests at heart and you stay in touch. I've built my training and coaching business over the last 14 years this way and I can tell you it really works.

In the next chapter I'll show you how to stay more in your 'flow' so you can grow…

Growing your sales flow

Now that you have an overview of the four energies and the eight profiles, it's important to understand that your goal is to be working in a company, sales team and sales role that puts you in your sales flow more of the time.

Put simply, flow is your path of least resistance. You'll recognise it as it's often a time when you are focused, know the goals you are trying to achieve, are having fun and are being highly productive.

When you are in a sales team in flow, productivity increases, results improve dramatically, there is far more positive energy and you feel more connected to the organisation.

The results can be spectacular as the business accelerates its sales performance and profits.

How much in flow (or out of flow) are you today?

To help you answer that we've created a short self-evaluation questionnaire for you to find out. You can download more copies for your sales team at
www.paulavins.com/salesflow.

This tool gives you a simple and measureable way to see the ten areas that impact your sales flow factor the most, enabling you to identify the key areas to focus on.

An important key is to link your own flow with how you build trust with customers and prospects to generate sales. We'll cover this in detail in the next few chapters.

Review this tool every quarter on your own and yearly with your manager or team to reflect and refine your training needs to improve performance.

On a scale of zero to ten, rate the following areas, based on zero being not true/not complete, through to ten being true/ complete.

Mark your level for each of the ten questions in the boxes.

1 I have clarity on what sales activities get me in flow and out of flow...

| 0 | 1 | 2 | 3 | 4 | 5 | 6 | 7 | 8 | 9 | 10 |

2 I focus all my time on activities that are in my flow and ask the team for help with others not in my flow...

| 0 | 1 | 2 | 3 | 4 | 5 | 6 | 7 | 8 | 9 | 10 |

3 I am able to build high levels of Trust & Rapport with Prospects...

| 0 | 1 | 2 | 3 | 4 | 5 | 6 | 7 | 8 | 9 | 10 |

4 I am excited about the coming year and what I will achieve and experience...

| 0 | 1 | 2 | 3 | 4 | 5 | 6 | 7 | 8 | 9 | 10 |

⑤ I consistently convert Prospects into Customers with Confidence & Conviction…

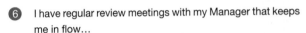

⑥ I have regular review meetings with my Manager that keeps me in flow…

⑦ I have a clear understanding of the Sales Process and where I add the most value…

⑧ I am in a company and industry that allows me to succeed & grow from my talents…

⑨ I am good at consistently following up my Sales Opportunities…

⑩ I easily take unexpected opportunities and challenges in my stride…

TOTAL: Add up your scores. This is your score out of 100.

Now focus on which areas you want to increase.

Seek to make progress every time you invest time in doing this.

How you sell to your customers is more important than what you sell.

Sell Dynamo prospects on the new idea and the vision of how much better their lives will be after they own your product or service.

What inspires Dynamo buyers to buy now?

In this, the first of four chapters on the Talent Dynamics energies, we're going to talk about the Dynamo energies and the three types of profiles that are largely driven by this energy. You will find out exactly how to spot them and how to build trust with them before, during and after the sales meeting or presentation. I'll also cover what they like and what will kill sales with them so fast you'll wonder what happened.

Let's start by looking at how to sell to the Dynamo energy profiles at a high level before we go deeper into the specifics of each one.

Just to recap, the three Dynamo energies are Mechanic, Creator and Star.

Figure 6 Selling to Dynamo customers

How to sell to Dynamo energies?

What they need	New products, new ideas, fast results.
How to present to them	Visually, fast, high energy, big picture.
What question they ask	What is the best deal I can get?
How to communicate	Using visual words, instant access and results.
What's important to them	How to grow, being first, ahead of competitors, important, VIP.
Sales killers	Lots of detail, step-by-step implementation plans, lengthy and wordy brochures and copy, talking slowly and laboriously.

Now you have the high level overview we'll look in detail at what drives each of the three profiles within the Dynamo energy so you can connect, communicate and convert more of them.

 Let's start with the purest form of Dynamo energy that is the **Creator** profile.

They're forward thinking, want the big picture and they like to move fast. They're often visionaries as they have an ability to see way beyond the present and into what will be happening two to five years from now.

They love new products, services and business opportunities. They're typically the early adopters in a product life cycle, whether it's Tesla cars, new iPhones or the latest marketing software, whatever will clearly help them to get one step ahead of their competition. They tend to want to buy in at the beginning, not at the end. This is key when evaluating which product to sell to them.

Creators are known for getting very excited in the moment when you are selling or presenting to them, as all they can see is the possibilities for themselves and their company. This passion and enthusiasm can be misread by other profiles as a definite decision to go ahead and purchase. However, five minutes after you leave they will be on to their next idea, opportunity or project.

One of the biggest challenges selling to this pure Dynamo energy can be getting what's sold implemented, as they tend to decide on their gut and then delegate to their teams, which can be awkward at times.

They also have a very short attention span, and they're distracted by bright shiny things and exciting limited offers. So, if your sales cycle takes too long, then the chances are they're going to have moved on before you've got them to the point of deciding.

 They just want the key facts so they can decide if it's relevant to their plans and future. If it is, great, if not they'll move on and they won't look back, so you really do get one chance with this type of person to make a high value impression.

One of our clients has a Dynamo Creator on her sales team. When we delivered this training for her, Chris shared how he had just purchased a house on impulse after walking past a sales board that said 'Move in for just £199 today.'

This shocked some of the other energy profiles in the team who thought it was crazy; however, if you need to make quick sales to hit your targets for the month or quarter, then contacting your Dynamo prospects will deliver you the fastest decisions and sales.

Sales manager tip

Make sure your sales people keep focusing on the new idea or product and the results customers will get quickly when they use it.

After all Dynamo green is for GO.

Be quick to show them the value in terms of how it's going to help them create new business or customers or help them to get new products to market or get ahead of their competition. They are motivated by future visions of success and results, and will only be motivated in solving today's problems when they are big enough to be almost shouting for their attention.

Your learning log

- What have you just discovered about Creator Dynamo profiles?
- Which of your current customers sprang to mind when you were reading this description?
- How will you change the way you interact with them as a result?

 Next, we'll be talking about the **Star** profile buyer, which is a mix of Dynamo and Blaze energy signified by the green and red in the icon.

They've got that celebrity personality, and they really do stand out. You will recognise them a mile off when you first meet them.

Star profiles love to be in the spotlight and love an audience, so make everything you say relevant to them and their future plans. They also love to talk and can frequently talk themselves into and out of buying during a meeting, while you've had very little time to talk at all.

You can often spot a Star as they tend not to like one-to-one conversations. If you're selling to them, they'll often want to get other people from their teams to sit in and listen to them talk to you about it.

They genuinely like to be seen as a charismatic leader at the front of the business, motivating and inspiring their people to growth and success.

The good news is that they are often very fast to spend their money, which can make them great for quick sales products and services.

They're good at building rapport with you if you happen to be a similar type of profile, but they like to buy products and services that enhance their position, either within the company, or their personal brand or stature as a mover or shaker in their market-place. They like to be seen as a high profile or a leading edge thinker in their industry.

 They aren't going to be interested in talking about efficiency gains or increases in productivity, in short anything that involves detail and reading. You'll know if you walk into the office of a Star profile, because they tend to have lots of pictures of themselves with famous or other successful people on their walls and they'll have awards or showcases in reception with success stories or press articles.

If you can point to your own company being at the front of your industry and winning awards, this will build trust with Stars. If you personally have won awards, even if it's just salesman of the quarter, don't be shy in sharing this with them as they like to associate with other successful people.

Let me demonstrate with a story of my own.

Wanting to attract new members for a coaching programme, we deliberately targeted companies of a certain size that had won industry awards. After he decided to work with me, one client in the physical security industry told me that he had checked me out on LinkedIn (www.LinkedIn.com/in/paulavins) and was impressed by the awards I had won and the business leaders I had spoken with on stage or worked with.

For this Star profile business owner, these two things built immediate trust with him and demonstrated that other people trusted me to deliver results. I worked with that client for over seven years and during that time his company went on to win many more industry awards and accolades, which made us both very happy.

Sales manager tip

When selling to a Star make sure your high Tempo and Steel profile salespeople become far more excited, expressive and engaging than they would normally feel comfortable with.

Warning. If you are going to work with Star Dynamos you need to be aware of several key things.

1 They can be high maintenance at times as it's all about them

② If you let them down they will hold a grudge for years and you will be unlikely to win back their business

③ At times, when under pressure, they will seem to get into attack mode and if you are on the receiving end of this it's a fairly painful experience

Your learning log

- What have you just discovered about Star Dynamo profiles?
- Which of your current customers sprang to mind when you were reading this description?
- How will you change the way you interact with them as a result?

 Finally, in the Dynamo energy we have the **Mechanics**.

Mechanics will want to know the how. They're very detailed people. They will want lots of product information and services, and will ask lots of 'how does this work?' questions. They want details on how your product or service will help them to fix or improve something they already have.

If you're trying to sell a big idea or a big concept, this can sometimes become frustrating. The key thing here is, if you are selling to a technical market, try to use a salesperson who is more Mechanic driven because they'll talk the right language naturally.

There's a whole process we teach clients in our training for matching and mapping the skills and the profiles in their team to the type of clients they're selling to.

Because Mechanics are more internal thinkers, they sometimes find it very hard to communicate their ideas to others on the team. They think things through in their heads until they have it perfect before giving feedback. This can create challenges in a sales presentation as you will get the lowest level of feedback and interaction from them of all the Dynamo profiles. However, when they do feed back get ready for lots and lots of detail and deep questions.

If you as the salesperson are more interested in relationships and talking, like a Deal Maker (see later), then responding to Mechanics can be very challenging as they will only buy with the right level of detail to build their trust.

All the Dynamo profiles are more visual than the other energies and Mechanics prefer to draw things out in meetings to understand how it all works. If you give them visual stimulus they usually respond well to that, but they'll always look at your product and service, and tell you what you can do to improve it, which can rub some of the other profiles up the wrong way.

This can sometimes come across as negative and may make salespeople and entrepreneurs feel that Mechanics are just criticising what they are doing. They're not. It's just the way that they add value inside their businesses and their organisations, by taking something and improving it, and that's just the way they see work.

Sales manager tip

When selling to a Mechanic make sure your high Blaze and Tempo energy salespeople give them enough detailed plans and proof that what you are selling works.

If you're in discussions with a potential client who is talking about how it works, asking all sorts of detailed questions about the operations, how it functions and is always coming up with ideas for you (you'd make it better by doing this, make it better by doing that), then it's a pretty good indication you're talking to a Mechanic, and you're going to want to adopt a different strategy when selling to them.

They need a mix of new ideas and facts to make decisions on. Ideas alone are not enough because their Steel energy will want detail to help to drive their decision.

Your learning log

- What have you realised about selling to Mechanic profiles?
- Which of your current customers sprang to mind when you were reading this description?
- How will you change the way you interact with them as a result?

Now that we've covered the three Dynamo energies, let's talk about how to use Dynamic Selling™ to generate trust before, during and after the sale.

Of course it's harder to spot a buying energy before you've met them, so for this section we'll assume you've had prior contact with the buyer either in person, while networking, at a trade show or on the phone.

Before the sale

The key is not to bombard them with lots of pre-meeting information, as they will either leave it to the very last minute or they'll not make time to review it, so this adds little or no value.

Be sure to connect with them on LinkedIn so that you can see the key relationships you have in common, which is great with

Star profiles, as well as looking at previous roles to see if they were more structured or creative. It's also a good idea to look through their website, Twitter feeds and so on, to see what awards they may have won and what their main focus is right now, or what topics they see as important.

A great tip here is to text them the day before saying you are looking forward to the meeting and to remind them of the time and location. This is because Creators and Stars have a habit of forgetting details like this and Mechanics will appreciate the detail – so you win on all levels.

If you have ever turned up for a meeting only to be told the buyer has gone out or forgotten, chances are they were Dynamo energy who got distracted by the next shiny opportunity or project.

Your job is to remind them of the value they saw in your product or service so they show up to the meeting. It's hard to make a sale when you are the only one in the room.

During the sale

Dynamo energy customers want lots to see, and lots of energy and excitement from you. Don't be afraid to share your passion for your product or service as it sells. Be sure to share big picture benefits and pay-offs in the future. Give the buyer the key bullet points and problems you solve for them followed by the best benefits you have.

Don't be too slow, methodical or get too detailed, that will turn Creators and Stars right off. The question they'll ask the most is, what's next? What are we going to do after we own this?

They haven't even bought the thing that you're talking to them about, and already they're talking to you about what's next, so it's important that you are ready to outline a clear road map of what their customer journey looks like for them.

Sometimes as the salesperson you need to actually slow a Dynamo profile down as they can get too carried away. Focus them on committing to the first step and order with you. Then tell them they can jump up the next levels. Use phrases like, 'Let's kick off today and then we can talk about what's next at my next visit.'

Remember that they like pictures, visuals or nice glossy brochures so that they can 'see' themselves owning your product or service.

You need to sell where they're going next, not where they are today.

Where they are might be painful, but they'll want to talk about how great it's all going to feel and look in the future. You only use very visual language:

- Can you see how fantastic this is going to be when it's implemented?
- Can you see how this will move your company forward?
- How does it look to you six months from now owning this?

What's most important to them is how to grow their business and be seen to grow and develop themselves. They will also want to be seen as being ahead of their competition, and you will need to make them feel like a very important customer. Of course, all customers should feel important, but it's particularly important for Dynamo energies.

If you want to upsell or cross sell products to Dynamos, the best time is when they are in the buying mode, as once a Dynamo starts buying they want to go big. Remember that with their short attention levels, trying to get in front of them later to cross sell will be hard as they will be on to the next project and product.

Dynamos are all about moving forward, not looking back.

After the sale

Typically, you want to be saying things like, 'OK, great. Once you've agreed this high level overview, I'll work with your team so that you're not bothered with the detail.'

- Keep them informed about new products in development.
- Invite them to VIP experiences, product launches and client appreciation dinners or days to make them feel special.
- Make sure they can see the first pass of the newest products as you launch them; after all, they like to be seen as ahead of the pack so you'll make more sales.

Risks

If you give them detailed proposals, wordy brochures or step-by-step plans, they will simply put them aside or to the bottom of the pile and procrastinate. They want to move quickly to make decisions.

Sometimes you can lose a sale to them, because somebody else comes in with a bigger, brighter, shinier object that they can buy right now, and they don't have to wait.

Five action steps

1. Take time to identify and list five current customers who you recognise as Dynamo energy buyers.

2. If you are a high Tempo profile sales person, Deal Maker, Trader or Accumulator, make sure you significantly raise your energy and level of excitement when working with Dynamo buyers.

3. If you are a high Steel profile sales person, Accumulator, Lord or Mechanic make sure you avoid going into too much detail with Dynamo buyers. Be more enthusiastic than you feel comfortable with and be OK to move to a decision quickly.

4. To speak a Dynamo buyer's language, make sure you focus on the big picture and keep your proposals and presentations short and to the point so they can make a quick decision.

5. If you don't know your Talent Dynamics profile yet then go to www.paulavins.com/profileoffer (to save £20 with code 'TD book offer').

If you want to win a £50,000 client you need to build a £50,000 relationship.

Blaze customers value the time you spend with them.

Who do Blaze buyers like to buy from?

In this chapter we are going to focus on how to sell to the three Blaze energy profiles. The Star, Supporter and Deal Maker are on the right-hand side of the Talent Dynamics square and are represented in red, because it's all about heart, warmth, relationships and people. Let's start with a high level overview.

Figure 7 Selling to Blaze customers

How to sell to Blaze energies?

What they need	Connection, time, relationships, variety.
How to present to them	Talking, stories, chatty, friendly, relaxed.
What question they ask	Who else have you worked with?
How to communicate	Get everybody involved, social proof, case studies, lots of contact and chatting.
What's important to them	Time and humanity, other people close to them, friendships and fun.
Sales killers	Using lots of detailed analysis with numbers and graphs, having to read things instead of discussing them, not engaging them in the eye and no smiling.

The Blaze buying profiles love people, relationships and variety so as customers they can be a lot of fun to sell to and work with.

They're often easy to spot if you go to a networking meeting or a sales presentation because they're the chatty ones, the vibrant outgoing people who want to talk about the social as well as the business side of life.

They'll want to build rapport very quickly with you, so it's important to talk about yourself as a person not just as a salesperson or as a businessperson. This is where understanding how to use the Triangle of Trust™ is so important (see page 30). Blaze energies trust in you when they know about your professional credibility and your humanity, what makes you tick.

This is where traditional sales training has always focused: first build rapport with the customer. In the case of Blaze buyers this is totally true, although it's not always true for some of the other energies, as you'll see later on.

Let's start by looking at how you identify this type of customer and how you actually spot them.

 We talked about Star energy customers in the last chapter, as they are a mix of Blaze and Dynamo energies. I'll give you a few key pointers here, but first go back and reread the Star section now.

- They love an audience and they like to talk a lot.
- Sales meetings and presentations with Stars will often last far longer than you budget and plan for.
- It can be a challenge to keep them focused and keep them coming back to the key points, because they'll love to go off, tell stories and hold an audience.

- They can lose track of time and suddenly the meeting ends because they've got to be somewhere else in a hurry and you never got to conclude the sale.

- They like to talk fast and spend their money fairly quickly when they see the value in a product or solution or the variety and excitement in the form of new experiences and fun.

- They love to connect with others, they love to be around others and they're great 'people people'.

- They like products that get them attention or enhance their position as a market-leading brand, company or individual – anything that will put them in a good light or point a spotlight at what they are doing.

Sales manager tip

Blaze customers like Stars want variety so let your salespeople present and work with them in different locations. Their office boardroom first time, over lunch second, at your offices with team tour for connection, social days out at races and so on. Keep them guessing and excited and remember that when they get bored they can change to a new supplier.

Your learning log

- What have you just discovered about Star Blaze profiles?

- Which of your current customers sprang to mind when you were reading this description?

- How will you change how you interact with them as a result?

 Next we have the **Supporter** profiles, typified by the heart. These buyers are fundamentally great with people and their teams usually love working for them and hold them in high regard and respect.

These are people whose entire way of operating is to think all about the people around them and not about how it will necessarily benefit them personally. They will put clients and their team first, above their own personal gain.

When you're selling to them it is critical you talk about the benefits to their team and perhaps their suppliers and of course their family. They usually have a very strong sense of fairness so they'll want to know that you operate from similar core values as a company and as a person.

They're very much about win/win and not about win/lose deals. They love to chat, love to socialise, love to spend time connecting, but they can be distrusting until they have spent quality time with you.

 They can have lower Steel and Dynamo energies, so planning may be a weakness. If planning is their responsibility, then you may find that sales or projects get stalled. They are often not very good at seeing the plan, and love to have it given to them. If you tell them how everything is going to work, they will feel a great deal more confident.

Once they buy in they tend to be great advocates. They are usually really good at just getting on with the job of getting it done, so they get a real result from your product and your service.

Often great testimonials come from Supporter clients who really love what you do. Because they're Supporters, they'll be supportive of you and if the product does exactly what you said it would and they get great results from your service, they will tell a lot of people about it. They usually have extensive social networks to promote you to.

Sales manager tip

When selling to a Supporter make sure your high Steel energy salespeople spend enough time building a rapport and relationship with the buyer and their team, as the team around the buyer needs to be on board for them to go forward. Too much focus on facts, figures and details will derail the sale.

Your learning log

- What did you just discover about Supporter Blaze profiles?
- Which of your current customers sprang to mind when you were reading this description?
- How will you change how you interact with them as a result?

Invest your time, energy and heart serving your future customers.

 Let's talk about the **Deal Maker** customers, who are a mix of Blaze and Tempo energies.

This type of buyer has a powerful mix of being able to build and leverage their relationships and networks and being tuned into what's happening in the market right now. The result is that they are usually able to get the best deal for their business from suppliers.

- They know *who* to ask for advice on the best supplier.
- They know *when* to place their order to get the best price.
- They function better in one-to-one situations and therefore generate high levels of trust with people, often getting hold of information not readily available in the marketplace.
- They don't like to be rushed, so will take their time buying until it's the perfect opportunity for the deal they want.

- They'll be very active on platforms like LinkedIn and Facebook because they're all about joining the dots and connecting.

You'll often find Deal Makers are on the phone. They're always doing deals and looking for angles.

They do like to operate with some structure and clear timings. So when you have meetings with them, combine tools such as meeting outlines and objectives with rapport and relationship building conversations.

Remember that this energy likes social selling. Let me tell you a story as an example.

 A few months ago I was introduced to a potential partner in New Zealand who was interested in licensing our trusted selling training programmes and courses. I knew his Talent Dynamics profile was a Deal Maker, so face-to-face time was going to be very important for him. Not so easy when we were on opposite sides of the world.

I found out when he was next in the UK for business and suggested he come and stay with me and my family so we could get better acquainted and see if we were a good fit. I vividly remember our first three hour dinner when we talked about our families, sales backgrounds, passions and visions for our lives. Only after we had done all this did we move on to discussing how we could add value to each other. Part of this was cultural as New Zealand is a very Blaze energy culture, whereas the UK is mainly Dynamo, but it was also a reflection of his profile.

The result is that we have developed a deep relationship over a number of calls and visits and have planned to launch my training into the Australian and New Zealand markets when we officially launch the new Talent Dynamics for Sales Profiles in 2017.

The biggest challenge is that quite often Deal Maker buyers like to avoid conflict. Their network is their lifeline so they are often seen as people pleasers. This can waste a lot of your time, so just be aware of it and give them permission to be honest with you even if it's to tell you 'no thanks'.

In my experience Deal Makers tend not to love technology. Spreadsheets and customer relationship management systems are a fast turn-off as they find them impersonal and unfriendly. They would rather go and talk to somebody in their network to get advice and input than work on their own to evaluate your product or service. If your presentation involves these kind of tools you may want to sit down and talk them through it to get the best from them.

Sales manager tip

When selling to a Deal Maker I suggest giving your sales-person permission to wine and dine them to help secure the sale. Social selling is always the preferred way for a Deal Maker to do business.

Your learning log

- What have you just discovered about Deal Maker Blaze profiles?

- Which of your current customers sprang to mind when you were reading this description?

- How will you change how you interact with them as a result?

Let's talk about how to sell to the Blaze energies and look at what they need and what they love before, during and after your sales presentation.

Before the sale

In order for you to build trust with Blaze energy buyers you have to invest your time in their emotional bank account. The more positive deposits you can make before you sit down with them, the better the chances they will trust you enough to do business with you.

Be sure to touch base with them via email, text and phone in the days and weeks before you sit down with them. I always suggest that clients have a system in place to bridge what I call the 'rapport gap', which is the time between making the appointment and the day you meet up.

You might also send them links to case studies and client success stories on your website, as this will show them that they are not the first person to try your product or service.

Remember that they love variety and they love relationship time, so, if you're engaging in pre-sales conversations, change it up a bit, try different locations or take them out for lunch, or to corporate hospitality events. If you can arrange for them to meet an existing client over lunch or out networking this is always a huge win.

During the sale

The best way to present to them is to talk with them. For them it's about relationship time, face-to-face time. I've had clients who have got on airplanes and flown to other countries, as they knew that if they sat in front of these clients and built relationships, they would win the business.

Use plenty of customer stories when explaining how your product or service works. Blaze customers usually love stories, and in a very informal, friendly and chatty environment.

The kind of questions they ask are 'who' questions.

They're about people, so they're always going to ask, 'Who have you worked with before? Who's done it? Who in your company would I be dealing with?'

They'll be asking, 'Who have you done business with in my industry?' or 'Who in our space?' They'll be looking for other reference points, such as others who have relationships with you they may tap into and ask about you. It's important to be aware that, if they're asking the 'who' questions, it's not an objection necessarily, it's just where their energy will default to. It helps you to identify them, but be ready to answer honestly. If you have customers you are both connected to via platforms like LinkedIn, now is the time to bring it up.

When communicating with them, it's really important to use things like case studies and social proof. Tell them about who else is using the product. They're not going to be the early adopters. Blaze energy buyers are more likely to come in when they can see other people have been there first.

Important to them are questions such as 'How will my team be impacted?' 'Are you in it for the long-term relationship?'

They want to see a long-term relationship track record, if possible. They want to see more than just a transactional experience. They want to know what's going to happen afterwards: who's going to stay in touch with them? Who's going to manage their relationship?

It's also very important for them to see how their existing suppliers may be impacted; their sense of fairness is very strong. They would hate to feel that an existing supplier could miss out. Even if they're moving to you and getting a better deal, they don't want to feel like they're letting anyone down.

They want to know how the team will be impacted, who in their business particularly will feel things, and they want to avoid any of those negative issues because they don't do conflict. You will need to work to mitigate any impact changing supplier to you may bring.

Avoid using lots of detailed analysis, lots of numbers and graphs or forcing them to read long proposals or documents, as these will really stop sales with them. They will prefer to sit down and talk it all through with you.

A number of clients we've trained have used this to massive effect. Rather than sending their proposals out by email (as quite often happens today), they have taken their future clients out and sat down face to face, maybe over a lunch or in some sort of social environment, and walked them through the proposal, discussing it and really connecting on a human level.

The key here is that they need to feel that you're engaging with them, so things like good eye contact are very important, as are positive facial gestures such as smiling and any cues that you're very happy to be around them. They want it to be social and they want it to be fun as well.

After the sale

It's important to remember that one of the main worries or concerns Blaze energy buyers have is that they will be neglected or forgotten after the sale. So stay in regular contact with them post-sale.

Send them a handwritten thank you card or gift. In the digital world we all operate in, this can have a huge positive impact. We do this with all our training and coaching programmes when we welcome a new customer into our community. Depending on the type of programme they have purchased and their energy type, we send a small gift and it means the world to people.

Schedule in follow-up calls – 30 days, 60 days and 90 days after the product or service has been delivered, so that they know you care.

As the old saying goes, 'People don't care how much you know until they know how much you care.' This is true for Blaze energy profiles more than any other.

Risks

Dropping the level of contact post-sale to focus on the next new business opportunity.

Delivering a poor product or service that does not meet their perceived expectations. Remember that they tend to have very large networks and if they are not happy with you or what they have purchased from you, they will have no issue telling everybody they know.

Not fully involving their team in all communications, especially if moving to you as a supplier will cause them some disruption or upset. They will already be feeling guilty about letting down their current supplier.

Five action steps

1. Take time to identify and list five current customers who you recognise as Blaze energy buyers.

2. If you are a high Dynamo profile sales person, Mechanic, Creator or Star you may need to slow down a bit for Supporters and Deal Makers so they don't feel overwhelmed and confused.

3. If you are a high Steel profile sales person, Accumulator, Lord or Mechanic, make sure you avoid going into too much detail with Blaze buyers. Spend more time being chatty than you usually do as they want to get to know you as a person they can trust and have a relationship with.

4. To speak a Blaze buyer's language, make sure you focus on their people and the benefits to the team involved. Use case studies, client stories and testimonial videos to raise the level of emotional connection and belief in you.

5. If you don't know your Talent Dynamics profile yet then go to www.paulavins.com/profileoffer (to save £20 with code 'TD book offer').

When do you ask Tempo buyers for the order?

Next we're going to talk about selling to Tempo energy customers.

In this chapter I'll walk you through how to sell to the three different profile types – Accumulator, Trader and Deal Maker.

We will be using the three steps of the sale we've already covered – before, during and after – so that you understand how best to add value at each stage.

First an overview of the key points for those who like the big picture before detail (Figure 8).

Figure 8 Selling to Tempo customers

How to sell to Tempo energies?

What they need	Connection, process, time, support.
How to present to them	Kinaesthetic, experience for themselves.
What question they ask	When do I need to decide?
How to communicate	Timely, steady pace, step-by-step plans.
What's important to them	Go at their pace, organisation, fairness.
Sales killers	Turning up late, fast talking, big ideas, not listening to their concerns, applying time pressured, 'decide today'.

To differentiate Tempo energy customers from the rest, here are some clues to help you spot them.

They absolutely live in the here and now. They're very focused on the present, tuned into their environment and have their ear to the ground in terms of what is happening right now.

If you're trying to sell to them based on a problem they haven't got yet, you'll struggle because they're interested in the problem they've got today. These are the clients that, if they've got a problem today, are more likely than not to order right now if you can prove your product or service solves it.

They love to tick things off their lists and complete projects and plans. A great question to ask them in a meeting is, 'Are you the type of person that likes lists that you tick off?' A more creative profile will have ideas all over the place on lots of bits of paper.

In contrast, a Tempo energy will be very organised. They will know exactly when they have to have replies back to people, decisions made and plans in place.

You'll also notice in meetings that go on longer than planned or agreed, that they'll start to twiddle with their pen and even start to get frustrated because they're not doing the next thing on their list that they had planned to be on to by now. Missing these clues in a sales meeting can literally destroy all the trust you may have previously built up.

Tempos tend to keep their stresses to themselves until they reach crisis point, at which time they may blow up on a phone call or on social media. So if they're very frustrated about something, you're not going to know about it as a supplier. In fact often the first you will know about it even being a problem is when they email you to say they're about to move to a competitor.

They are really big on fairness in how they are dealt with and deal with others. It's also really important that unplanned changes don't happen without them being consulted, as this will cause maximum stress levels at the speed of light.

So, if you're going to change any element of the product or service that you're going to be delivering, it's critical that you consult your Tempo customers all the way through. Even if changes prove to be unnecessary, the constant communication will build trust. Silence creates mistrust and worry and ultimately may cost you a customer.

 We spent quite a lot of time talking about the **Deal Maker** energy at the end of the Blaze chapter as this is a mix of both Tempo and Blaze.

If you jumped ahead to this chapter you may want to go back and read that section in more detail.

For now here is a quick reminder of the key points to remember when selling to a Deal Maker profile:

- Like to listen more than talk.
- Have great networks and relationships to tap into.
- Prefer one-to-one meetings and relationships than group dynamics.
- Enjoy mixing socialising with business, either networking or at events.
- Great negotiators as they know when and who will give them the best deal.
- Often the peacemakers as they dislike conflict and want everybody to get along.

Sales manager tip

When selling to a Deal Maker make sure that Steel sales people invest more time building connections. Invite them to events with networking opportunities as they'll love meeting new people one on one

Your learning log

- What have you just discovered about Deal Maker Tempo profiles?
- Which of your current customers sprang to mind when you were reading this description?
- How will you change how you interact with them as a result?

Next we have the **Trader**.

A Trader is not necessarily somebody who trades stocks and shares. What we're talking about is somebody who's very good at trading their time for other assets, results, influence or information.

They are always in the mindset of, 'If I give you this, you give me that.'

You'll recognise them in any kind of negotiations because they'll always be trying to trade something off. If you want something, they're going to want something in return. They're going to try and say, 'How about I give you this and, in exchange, you'll give me that.' Some people have learnt this as a technique, while Traders are naturally very good at it.

They've got a great sense of timing and balance of priorities and are able to look at what's right and what's wrong. They are big on ticking things off their list and hate going home with 'to-dos' not done as it makes them feel they have let their customers or team down.

Traders are great as they can prioritise quickly and see what will have the biggest impact right now. They are the exact opposite of the Dynamo 'talkative' salesperson stereotype as they move at a much slower pace. They want a step-by-step plan and need to complete things before moving on.

They generally don't like to be out in front of people and prefer to be the power behind a more outgoing profile. That's totally the case in my business where my business manager Lesley (Trader) does a great job of making sure everything happens on time for all our customers, trainers and delegates.

When selling to a Trader I suggest using a lot of detail and view it as a multi-step sales process.

Your learning log

* What have you just discovered about Trader Tempo profiles?
* Which of your current customers sprang to mind when you were reading this description?
* How will you change how you interact with them as a result?

 Finally, we have the **Accumulators**.

Accumulators want lots of information before making a decision. They can be seen as more pessimistic than optimistic, because they're only happy to move forward if they've got all the relevant information. They will be very cautious if they have purchased a similar product or service to yours before and they were let down by the supplier or it didn't live up to the 'sales promises'.

One of the worst things you can do with Accumulators is to push them into a quick decision.

To build trust with an Accumulator, you invest time, happily and willingly, to demonstrate your commitment to them and solve an immediate painful problem they have today. This adds huge value in advance and builds up trust quickly.

Let me give you an example from my own coaching business.

A business owner and his wife were interested in joining my F12 Mastermind coaching programme. He was definite he wanted to join, but she was very nervous as they had worked with other 'sales coaches' before and been left out of pocket and with team problems (unfortunately not an uncommon story in my industry). So I invested time with this couple after an event to work with them privately to solve a very pressing business problem they had. The result was that after taking some time to think it over, they joined the Mastermind and have been great members ever since.

It's important to realise that Accumulators have a genuine fear of making a wrong decision. Some of this is because they also have a fair amount of Steel energy, hating to waste time, money or effort. Having to go back and do something again is very painful for them.

This is why they do a lot of research to try and eliminate making the wrong decisions. The challenge sometimes is they spend all their time researching and don't actually make any decisions at all. This will really frustrate Dynamo salespeople who want quick decisions so that they can move on. This often costs them sales that they would have got if they had learned to either slow down or pass it to a team member whose profile is better suited to working with Accumulators.

Accumulators are really good project managers. You'll often find them in roles like HR or compliance or health and safety, where they've got to get things right.

You will find that whatever they're doing, there's a high level of processing and compliance in what they do and how their business operates. They also tend to buy into reassurance and support that they're getting it right.

They don't want to be rushed; they want to take it slowly and be sure to make the right decision. Look out for these kind of clues in their language. Accumulators like a lot of detailed information before making up their minds. You may have an initial scoping meeting and then want to give them lots of relevant information and research paths for them to take before asking them to sign anything.

Sales manager tip

When selling to an Accumulator buyer make sure your high Dynamo salespeople take it much slower than normal as they may rush the sale and push the buyer away. They will also need to bring more Steel energy and give the buyer plenty of detail to do their research before asking for the order.

Your learning log

- What have you just discovered about Accumulator Tempo profiles?
- Which of your current customers sprang to mind when you were reading this description?
- How will you change how you interact with them as a result?

Now we'll look at how to sell to the Tempo energies and at what they need and what they love before, during and after your sales presentation.

Before the sale

It always builds trust to confirm the time and date of the meeting a few days before it's due. The Tempo buyer will probably know it already, but it's important to demonstrate to them that you value their time.

Take time to plan out your journey in advance. I know it sounds obvious, but trust me, most salespeople try to cram in too much and often leave things like planning to the last minute. If a Tempo buyer is visiting your offices, remember that they will be early, every time.

I'll often send a short agenda with start and finish times clearly displayed so they know how much time they are investing in the meeting. However, remember that whatever you put down it's essential you stick to it, even if your sales presentation is not done. Overrunning is a huge sign of disrespect for their most valuable asset, their time. You'll never win a sale when you do this.

Arrive early for the meeting. This demonstrates you respect their time and your own.

During the sale

The first thing they need is a real sense of connection to you as a person.

They need to know that they're going to get a great amount of support once they become a customer of yours. This is really important for them, so you need to support them a lot during the buying decision.

You need to be available to answer their questions. You need to be there for them, and as a result of that they feel confident and trust you more. It's important that you sell the benefits of your post-service support and customer care plan. Without this, even if your product is better than your competitor's, you'll not win the order.

Tempo buyers don't like to make quick decisions and it can destroy all trust they have in you if you insist on 'a decision today', as a lot of old school sales training still teaches.

It's also important for the buyers to get an 'experience' of your product or service before they buy. They like to learn and process through a physical experience, not just pictures or words, so think of ways to make your product or service come alive.

These are very touchy-feely energies. They want to get their hands on it. If it's a product, they're going to want to hold it physically. At the very least, put a brochure in their hands in a meeting – or something that will allow them to feel that they're involved. It's very important that you don't present *at* them. Instead, involve them in any presentation you make. They can't make appropriate judgements if they can't feel anything.

I have a printer coaching client who wanted to win a huge contract with a big motor manufacturer. However, the buyer didn't want to risk making a bad decision and leaving their current supplier. We eventually persuaded him to come to the factory for half a day and see the processes my client had in place. He also got to meet the team that ran the machines and to build up the trust that they could deliver on time, every time for him. He handled all the products, played with all the inks, even set up a machine himself. He really got involved with how everything worked.

What was the return on this investment of time and effort? Well, when the contract was next up for renewal they got to bid and won over £250,000 of new work.

Don't think you are wasting time with Tempo customers; you're actually investing it so be sure to invest in value building experiences.

They tend to ask when and where a lot during the sales process. When's it going to be delivered? Where's it coming from? When will we expect to get a return on this? Where are the timelines?

Where will the support come from? When will we get what we have been promised? Look out for those key questions because they turn up a lot.

It's important that you go at their pace and they also want to feel that there's a high level of organisation and fairness. They want to know that they're getting value for money, and the only way they're going to know that is if they go out and talk to your competitors. Often they'll want to do that research. It's really important that you're able to let them do that and understand that it's part of their process. It's not a reflection on you, your product or your company. It's just their buying process, so don't take it personally.

The best way to win the order is to ask them, 'When would you like to take a test drive?' 'When would you see this printer being installed?' Use questions that bring in the timing element because if they are genuinely interested they will have already been thinking about the time implications and will have a detailed answer for you.

After the sale

A great tool you can use is to give the customer a checklist of things they should go away and research.

Send them any quotes you promised earlier than promised – always under-promise and over-deliver. Send them useful links to help them with their research, even if it's to other companies' websites or to expert sources.

Offer to have them talk with your technical support people to get their more detailed questions answered, or offer to bring a technical expert back with you if relevant.

Follow up on time with answers to questions they may have. Have clear step-by-step instructions and implementation guides you can send them to demonstrate you've done this many times before and that they are in safe hands.

Finally, let them talk to a customer who's had similar concerns. You may do this while they come to your offices for a visit or, even better, you could take them to visit the site of a customer happily using your product.

The key point here is make sure there are no surprises and that you are following a plan you agreed with the customer. Trust flows from time together and ticks the boxes.

Risks

Turning up late absolutely destroys trust immediately even if it's not your fault, and will kill deals with this kind of energy and these three profiles. I had a client drive all the way from London to Manchester for a meeting with a large new client and got stuck for two hours on the M1 after an accident and lost the business. Yes he called ahead a number of times from the car, but the buyer was just not interested when he arrived. Not perhaps fair but it was an interesting learning experience for my client.

The next risk is behaving like a typical fast-talking salesperson. This will really cause Tempo buyers problems and they will be highly distrustful of you. In the desire to close the sale, do not, and I repeat, do not speed up the process or try to go quicker.

A further risk is not delivering when you say and on what you promise. This is really important; the quickest way to destroy trust with a Tempo energy customer is to over-promise and under-deliver. These kind of things destroy the trust incredibly quickly, and you're only ever going to be trying to play catch-up.

Take care with Tempo customers not to be distracted by things like mobile phones and social media or anything that takes you away from being fully present with them. Again, this can destroy trust and kill deals because they may feel that you are not fully with them in the here and now, and that's where they operate.

Also, riding roughshod over their objections. If they give you an objection it's not a good idea to say to them, 'Oh, don't worry about that.' You need to understand what they're worried about and what the impact is they're concerned about. Try to help them unpack it and get into the details so that they can comfortably talk through a way to get to a conclusion of 'OK, yeah, I can see how that can work.'

Five action steps

1. Take time to identify and list five current customers who you recognise as Blaze energy buyers.

2. If you are a high Dynamo profile sales person, Mechanic, Creator or Star, you'll need to think in terms of taking the sale step by step with Deal Makers, Traders and Accumulators so they don't feel overwhelmed and pressured. Give them time to do their research and deliver on your promises.

3. Tempos value their time so always be early for meetings.

4. To speak a Tempo buyer's language makes sure you focus on the service and support they'll receive. They hate to make a wrong decision and need to be sure you can deliver.

5. If you don't know your Talent Dynamics profile yet then go to www.paulavins.com/profileoffer (to save £20 with code 'TD book offer').

If you don't have a system for selling, you'll always be at the mercy of your prospect's system for buying. – David Sandler

Steel buyers respond best to a structured sales presentation packed with data and facts.

How do you secure a Steel buyer's business?

In this chapter we're going to talk about the Steel energy profiles and customers. We will discover how to sell and connect with Accumulators, how to connect and sell to Lords, and how to connect and sell to Mechanics.

First let's start off with the high level overview (Figure 9). Steel energy buyers are often the most misunderstood in my experience, often being referred to as 'negative' by salespeople with more Dynamo or Blaze profiles. Actually, they're not, but traditional sales training telling you to spend 20 minutes building rapport may actually lose you a sale with a Steel buyer.

Let me show you why...

Figure 9 Selling to Steel customers

How to sell to Steel energies?

What they need	Security.
How to present to them	Spreadsheets, data, detail.
What question they ask	How much will this all cost?
How to communicate	Focus on tasks, numbers and ROI.
What's important to them	Guarantees, results, proof, statistics, no risk factor.
Sales killers	New products, innovation, first to try, lots of social chat, not being able to answer detailed questions.

To differentiate the Steel energy customers from the rest, here are some clues to help you spot them, before, during and after the sale.

What they need, more than any other energy, is data, security and facts. They are very cautious buyers and will want to know exactly how everything works so that they feel safe buying your product or service.

They really don't like to buy early in a product's life cycle. They will usually try to wait until other people have been there before them, until it's proven and all the kinks and risks have been eliminated. Trying to sell a new product to them is very difficult and they won't go for it because there's no security. They're looking for things like guarantees, proof, case studies, data metrics and so on.

We spent quite a lot of time talking about the Accumulator energy at the end of the Tempo chapter, as they are a mix of both Tempo and Steel.

If you jumped ahead to this chapter you may want to go back and read that section in more detail.

For now here is a quick reminder of the key points to remember when selling to an Accumulator profile:

- They want lots of relevant information and research before making a decision.

- They can be seen as more pessimistic than optimistic, because they're only happy to move forward if they've got all the details and relevant information.

- They will be very cautious if they have purchased a similar product or service to yours before and they were let down by the supplier or it didn't live up to the 'sales promises'.

- One of the worst things you can do with Accumulators is to push them into a quick decision. This won't win their business, but will push them away from you.

- They don't like to make the wrong decision, as they don't like letting people down or wasting time.

- They like to buy from salespeople who have a lot of product knowledge as this builds trust.

Sales manager tip

When selling to an Accumulator profile buyer make sure that high Dynamo and Blaze sales people slow down and take the time to support them with their research. Let them go at their own pace and avoid using 'buy today' offers as these tend to destroy trust and lose customers.

How do you secure a Steel buyer's business?

Your learning log

- What have you just discovered about Accumulator Steel profiles?

- Which of your current customers sprang to mind when you were reading this description?

- How will you change how you interact with them as a result?

Remember that this type of buyer will accumulate, as their name suggests, a lot of information and background on you, your company, your product's features, benefits and flaws, as well as case studies. They will also want to know who has purchased from you and who hasn't.

This often means they are better informed than the majority of salespeople they meet, which just kills the deal dead. In fact in a recent trusted sales training workshop I ran for a client's team, one Accumulator told me how he had visited motor bike dealers to purchase a bike and left all four without buying. I asked him why. 'I knew more about their bikes and products than they did,' he said, 'so how could they add value to my decision making process?' A point very well made and one that all sales managers and business owners need to pay attention to. After all, that £12,000 purchase was already made in the customer's mind; he was just looking for somebody he could trust enough to place the order with and pay his deposit to.

As a recent survey discovered, over 52 per cent of a customer's buying decision is based on the experience of dealing with the salesperson. That being the case, surely it makes sense to spend over 50 per cent of a company's training budget on teaching salespeople how to build trusted relationships and not just focusing on the product, as this only impacts the sale by 19 per cent (Insidesales.com).

Accumulators are sometimes seen as a stumbling block or the person slowing the buying process down within a company because they want so much data and information.

Their biggest fear is of actually making the wrong decision and wasting time, money and brainpower. Those are three of the biggest things that really drive the Accumulator profile when purchasing. Make sure you are able to offer detailed product information and guarantees to de-risk the decision for them as much as possible. If you don't yet have a profit pulling guarantee in your business, then visit www.paulavins.com/guaranteebuilder and download my ebook giving you a step-by-step plan to implementing one that will double your sales.

 Next, we have the **Lord** profile.

Lords are, in my view, one of the easiest profiles to spot. They are all about the detail, data and 'how' your product or service will deliver a return and result for them. Often misunderstood as 'negative', they have a mindset that is all about mitigating risk and disruptive impact on their existing people, processes and plans.

Let me tell you a story to demonstrate what I mean.

I recently had a lunch with the management team of a small company looking to work with a business coach to accelerate their sales. I had just sat down at the table when I got hit with a barrage of questions from the financial and operations director about how I worked with clients like them. How long had I been coaching? How would my programme guarantee them more sales? How could I justify my prices? How would I impact their sales team?

Had I not known about the Trusted Selling System™, I may have been tempted to jump in and start answering these questions, which would almost certainly have lost their trust and proved to them that I didn't have a selling system.

Instead what I did was suggest we order some drinks and I then explained to them that I had a proven process I'd developed over 14+ years. I then went on to explain that this system had helped businesses just like theirs, told them that I wanted to take them through it now and this would answer all the questions they had just raised. That way they got all the details and data they were looking for to make the right decision and I got to see if they were a good fit for me as a client.

At the time of writing, I have been working with them for six months and together we have delivered record sales in the last quarter – and we are just getting warmed up. Their sales team is excited and motivated and productivity is already up 20 per cent so my Lord client is very happy.

 It's important to remember that Lord profiles usually don't like small talk, viewing it as a waste of time. They want to jump straight into the detail. The old school sales training approach of spending time building rapport, talking about family and hobbies and so on no longer works in this case.

Not all Lord profiles are created the same and the exception to this is when they also have high Blaze energy and Steel. This is very rare and I have so far only worked with one client with this type of profile, but it can be challenging as they swing from very friendly to very direct depending on the pressures they are under that day.

Remember that Lords are strong on detail and data, which is where they add a lot of value to a team, and they really like a structured approach to their working life. They want meetings to run to agendas. They want proof that their investment of time or money is going to give them a return. They want to know that they're not wasting their time talking to you, so they're going to need more convincing before they sit down and have an initial meeting with you.

They often have very little patience, especially with salespeople, and they will be looking for you to demonstrate your personal level of expertise and experience to build trust with them. This is a great opportunity to use the Triangle of Trust™ we talked about in Why trust beats tips, tricks and tactics.

Because Lords like so much detail, they tend to overcomplicate things and to be honest with you, are very direct in their communication style. They can sometimes be seen as rude or confrontational by other energies, especially Blaze and some Dynamos. I've often been on the end of two or three word emails from them, and as for a 'Hi, how was your weekend?', you're talking to the wrong profile.

If you're a Blaze salesperson, then you'll find Lords particularly challenging to sell to as your usual tools for building trust, talking about people, spending time with them, sharing stories and so on won't work. They just want you to get to the facts and fast.

Remember that the profile directly opposite your natural tendency is the one you tend to find the hardest to sell to because it's opposite to who you are and your core. So Tempo salespeople struggle with Dynamos as they just talk too fast and they are all over the place with no plan whatsoever.

Sales manager tip

When selling to a Lord buyer help Blaze salespeople be direct, detailed and data focused and less chatty. They will struggle the most and may become demotivated.

Your learning log

- What have you just discovered about Lord Steel profiles?

- Which of your current customers sprang to mind when you were reading this description?

- How will you change how you interact with them as a result?

Finally, there is the **Mechanic** profile.

We spent quite a lot of time talking about the Mechanic energy in What inspires Dynamo buyers to buy now? as it's a mix of both Steel and Dynamo energies.

You may want to go back and read that section in more detail. For now here is a quick reminder of the key points to remember when selling to a Mechanic profile:

- They think things through in their heads until they have it 'perfect' before giving feedback, so they can be frustrating to sell to.

- They are great at seeing an opportunity and how they can improve on it and make it better.

- They need to know you have a system and process that is proven to deliver returns and results.

- They are always looking to fix problems or streamline systems. They love to get information in visual formats that they can interact with. So use tools like iPads, whiteboards, Mind Maps.

- They love to get lots of product details, technical specs and analysis before purchasing.
- They will read every detail in your proposals all the way to the end, so get them right.
- They can be demanding post-sales customers as will only accept 'perfect' installation and so on, and can sometimes miss the bigger picture.
- They are not great negotiators as this is too high Blaze energy for them and people management is something they avoid.
- Expect them to delegate pre-sales meetings to others on their teams if there is a lot of discussion or scoping needed at any point in the sale. They will just want the one page overview at the end backed up by a detailed report for them to read on their own.

Sales manager tip

When selling to a Mechanic make sure your salesperson can work with more detail without losing patience. Mechanics need a mix of new ideas and facts to make decisions and respond really well to interactive presentation tools and visual aids.

Your learning log

- What have you just discovered about Mechanic Steel profiles?
- Which of your current customers sprang to mind when you were reading this description?
- How will you change how you interact with them as a result?

It's time to look at how to sell to the Steel energies and at what they need and what they love before, during and after your sales presentation.

Before the sale

Remember that they are going to be doing their research on you and your company before they meet you, so make sure all your profiles are fully up to date. There is nothing worse for a Steel energy buyer to see than a half finished LinkedIn profile. It gives them the impression you don't finish things and can't be trusted.

Email them with some links to detailed product information to review before you meet, as well as case studies that demonstrate a clear result for the customer.

During the sale

For maximum impact and trust, they need spreadsheets and data and lots and lots of detail and proof in any presentation you deliver. All three profiles, Accumulator, Lord and Mechanic, are internal thinking people, so don't expect to have a high energy meeting with lots of relationship building.

Steel energy profiles prefer to process decisions on their own and not include others in their thinking. They prefer to do that internally – usually on their own after you have left. They like to take information away and have the time to sit in peace and quiet and really process it.

This is why having the right collateral, brochures and so on is so important, even in today's digital world. I recently had a case when a managing director had attended an event of mine about my business growth accelerator programme, F12 Mastermind.

He was very enthusiastic about its potential, but his business partner, and wife, was not able to make it. He left the meeting with a detailed brochure though and took it home for her to read.

It transpired that she was a Lord profile and having read the ten pages of detail on 'how' the programme was constructed and the meetings run, and found out what they would get to take away for their business, they decided to join my next Mastermind without her ever meeting me in person.

This is the power of having the right tools to talk to the right energy of your buyer. Yes that brochure took me several days to write, but it's already given my business a ten times return on investment.

Always remember that detailed data drives their decisions to purchase.

It's important to remember that all the Steel profiles tend to generate this feeling of being blockers in a sales process or being negative towards what you are selling. Certainly if they're brought in as part of a buying team, they'll be the ones that are seen as slamming the brakes on and being awkward because all they ever do is ask how questions.

If you're a Dynamo profile and your selling style is very much 'big picture' and painting those pictures for customers, then dealing with a customer who's a Steel energy is going to put you absolutely up against somebody who is the complete opposite of everything you are about. Not big picture, but micro-picture detail, and they really want to delve into the specifics of how it's all going to work, which can be super frustrating.

To communicate with them, you've got to focus on the tasks, the detail, the numbers, the return on investment, the analysis, the proof and the data, and focus on the task at hand. Don't get seduced by the big picture. Don't jump too far ahead. Just focus on the next task with them and really work that through.

When deciding to order, guarantees and proof are important to them. They want statistics and, ultimately, they want to make sure that they're not putting their neck on the line and taking any kind of unnecessary risk. Of all the energies, they are the most risk-averse, so if there's no data, there's high risk. If there's data, it's low risk.

After the sale

Send them any information they asked for. If you don't know the answer to something don't try and 'fudge it' as these buyers want facts, and uncertainty damages trust in you.

Agree when they would like you to follow up with them and the best way – email, phone and so on.

Risks

Poor product knowledge and not being able to answer their detailed questions will potentially derail or kill sales with this kind of energy and these three profiles. What's critical here is that if you don't know the answer, be honest and transparent and say, 'I don't know, but let me go and find out and get back to you.' It really is important that when you do, you get them the detailed information they require. Don't come back with waffle, because that will destroy the trust that you have or that you're building with them.

These buyers are normally slower to make decisions so if you're looking to hit a target or a performance indicator for the month, they're not the buyers to chase down for quick decisions.

Five action steps

1. Take time to identify and list five current customers who you recognise as Steel energy buyers.

2. If you are a high Dynamo profile salesperson, Mechanic, Creator or Star, you'll need to think in terms of making the sale using a very structured format with Accumulators, Lords and Mechanics to make them feel safe and secure.

3. Steel buyers hate waste so don't waste their time with small talk as this destroys trust and adds no value. Instead get to the point and demonstrate cost or time savings with spreadsheets and facts.

4. To speak a Steel buyer's language make sure you focus on data, details and documents. They love to read all the details so bring brochures. They are usually the last to try a new product so focus on proven products rather than new releases.

5. If you don't know your Talent Dynamics profile yet then go to www.paulavins.com/profileoffer (to save £20 with code 'TD book offer').

91% of customers say they'd give referrals but only 11% of salespeople actually ask for them!

Dale Carnegie

Four ways to follow up for fortunes

Meeting a new potential customer is just the start of the relationship.

Now you know how to identify the four different types of buying energies, you can alter your sales presentation to match their preferred communication style. You'll know certain types are more likely to make quick decisions, while others need more time to reflect or research before buying.

So it's important that you know how to follow up with each of the four types of buying energies so that you move seamlessly from meeting a 'shopper' to winning a 'customer' to creating a 'raving fan'.

First, a key point to remember. I see so many salespeople give up on potential customers far too early just because their own profile may not like to wait or stay in touch (Figures 10 and 11). This is another great reason why you need to understand all the profiles in your team, so you can work together to maximise sales over the longer term.

Figure 10 Don't give up too early

67%

of prospective buyers who tell you 'no' today will be ready to buy in the next year.

Gartner research

Next 12 months

Figure 11 Stay in contact

80%

of leads you consider to be 'dead' will buy within 2 years if you stay in contact.

Sirus research

Within 2 years

How to follow up with the four buyer energies

Dynamo

- Fast. These buyers don't wait around.
- Typically give them 24 hours and they'll buy if they see an immediate value.
- Use technology like text and instant messaging to get their attention and decision.
- Remember that they will be on to their next project or supplier quickly.
- Take action now and follow up before it's too late.

Blaze

- Invest time with them to deepen the trust and relationship. Take them out for lunch to catch up. Involve them in social events, golf days, networking or customer site visits for social proof.
- Send them links to customer videos and case studies.
- Ninety-three per cent of all sales interaction happens via the phone, so make lots of quick calls to stay connected and trusted.
- Make sure you ask for referrals and introductions from your Blaze customers as they have the biggest networks.
- Have them meet other members of your company so they feel connected to your team and not just you.

Tempo

- Do what you said, when you said you would. This is vital for a Tempo energy buyer for trust to remain after the first meeting.

- Deliver them a step-by-step plan of how any implementation process would work.

- Agree on how often they would like you to stay in contact.

- Be sure to share your service level agreements (SLAs) with them.

- Play the long-term game and stay in regular contact until the time is right for them to purchase.

Steel

- Send lots of supporting detail and data in any proposals or tenders.

- Remind them of your personal credibility as they look to trust experts in areas where they don't have a background or experience.

- Let them speak to technical experts in your team to get more 'how' questions answered.

- Don't misread their silence as disinterested; they could just be digesting data.

- Communicate through platforms like LinkedIn and email rather than by phone, as they tend not to be the most chatty of customers.

About the author

Paul Avins MISMM is known as one of the most sought after sales growth experts, trainers and trusted advisors in the business world today. His 14-year track record of helping his clients and their teams achieve accelerated and sustainable growth in their companies has won him numerous awards and accolades.

He is sort after for his ability to create innovative strategic growth plans and programmes that drive his client's sales, profits and success goals, without high pressure sales tactics or short-term tricks and gimmicks.

His direct approach cuts through the management speak clichés to build high levels of trust with his clients, some of who have worked with him for over ten years. Paul's passion and commitment to get his clients and their teams to take massive consistent action has been getting impressive results for over 14 years in an industry that sees many so called sales experts come and go.

As a Talent Dynamics global partner and performance coach, Paul believes strongly in helping sales leaders and teams to tap into their talents and leverage their unique individual value to drive growth and exceed targets.

Paul's primary Talent Dynamics profile is a Creator (Dynamo) with secondary profiles of Mechanic and Star, which enables him to add huge value to the clients he serves.

A believer in teams, he has a great team backing him up in his office: Lesley his operations manager (Trader) and Becky his marketing manager (Lord), as well as an extended team of world class trainers and flow consultants who help to deliver his training programmes for clients across the world.

He's the creator of F12Mastermind.com, the UK's number one business mastermind for £1m+ businesses wanting to scale and sell over the next 2–5 years. This programme attracts driven business owners looking to push themselves and their teams to high levels of performance and profit.

Paul has written three best-selling books, *Business SOS* (Paul Avins Enterprises Ltd, 2009), *Secrets of the Wealth Accelerators* (Sunmakers, 2011) and *Mastermind Your Way to Millions* (Paul Avins Enterprises Ltd, 2015), and will be releasing his *The 5 Step Formula for Building your Dream Team* with Wiley in 2017.

At his core is his passion for sales and business development, having built and sold four companies by the age of 30, including several large sales teams. His constant drive to always be learning new skills and strategies puts him at the forefront of the industry. Behind this consistent commitment to his own self-development is a desire to distil and teach strategies and value to his clients to bring them faster results and returns.

Paul has been featured on the BBC and many local radio stations as a business expert providing comment and advice. He's also been featured in *The Daily Telegraph*, *The Franchise Magazine*, *Champions of Small Business* and *IN Business* to name just a few.

He is a sort after keynote speaker, working with clients including VW, 365 Salon Success, ECCO Shoes, Platinum Property Partners and so on, and has personally trained over 3,500 people in his career to date.

Paul's passion for trust-based selling has led him to be a leading speaker on the subject within the Institute of Sales and Marketing Management of which he's an active member.

Hard work always beats talent… If talent doesn't work hard!

Will Smith
actor and musician

A big thank you to...

Roger James Hamilton and Michelle Clark from Entrepreneurs Institute, without whose support this book would not have been possible.

Resources

www.talentdynamicsforteams.com

To connect with Paul visit any of the links below:

www.PaulAvins.com and www.PaulAvins.com/salespodcast

www.F12Mastermind.com

www.Linkedin.com/in/paulavins

www.facebook.com/paulavins

Twitter: @paulavins

Instagram: @paulavins

Email: p.avins@paulavins.com

Tel: +44 (0)1869 278900

If people like you, they'll listen to you.

But if they *trust* you they'll do business with you!

Zig Ziglar

Go further with our additional training

- Sales dynamics profiles and personal debrief
- Sales team growth acceleration days
- Triple your sales team sessions (2 hours)
- Team building recruitment and coaching
- Flow consultant certification (2 days)
- Performance consultant certification (3 days)
- All training includes up to £500 of free tokens
- Free profile tokens valid for 12 months
- Bulk book purchases for your team

Email team@td4teams.com or call +44 (0)1869 278900 and talk to Lesley.

Want to know how to boost your team's sales results? Call us today for a free 30 minute sales growth call with Paul Avins.

Also by Authority Guides

The Authority Guide to Financial Forecasting for SMEs: Pain-free financials for finance and planning
Simon Thompson

Build a better, faster forecast.

In this Authority Guide, forecasting guru Simon Thompson shows you how to build financial forecasts quickly, effectively and cheaply through his unique, proven and easy-to-follow 10-step process. By learning how to create effective forecasts you will master the ability to understand the potential financial outcomes for your business and be able to communicate financial information in order to successfully raise investment or loans.

The Authority Guide to Presenting and Public Speaking: How to deliver engaging and effective business presentations

Steve Bustin

Are you required to present, pitch or speak to an audience?

Whether it's your first presentation or you're an experienced speaker, this Authority Guide will give you the tools, tips and confidence to deliver engaging, creative and effective presentations. Steve Bustin, an award-winning business speaker (named UK Speaker of the Year 2015 by the Professional Speaking Association), an executive-level speech coach and corporate presentation skills trainer, will teach you some simple techniques to make sure your audience is engaged.

The Authority Guide to Publishing Your Business Book: Take your business to a new level by becoming an authority in your field
Sue Richardson

Are you ready to become a trusted advisor to the business world?

Publishing expert, Sue Richardson, shows you how to use your expertise, knowledge and experience to become a published authority in your field and gain the visibility you and your business needs. This Authority Guide will help you to create a plan that ensures you write and publish the right book for your business.